Transformative Leadership

The Core of Vision and Impact

A Visionary leader inspires and motivates those around them by painting a compelling picture of the future. Then they communicate their vision with passion and enthusiasm, igniting a sense of purpose and commitment throughout those around them.

ISAIAH IKE JOHNSON

ISBN Number:

9798302447760

Acknowledgments

Thanks to my family, the many leaders, co-workers and peers for their influence on my life and my career. The experience of interacting with them and spending time with each one has been priceless. You all have inspired me and helped me to be better in some way.

I am grateful to my wife Annette, of 49 years of marriage who allowed me the space to develop and grow as an individual and leader doing the things that I loved; developing, influencing, impacting and leading people to get things done; while developing and growing myself; "Iron sharpen iron."

Special thanks to Major General Cliff Stanley, one of the most professional and detailed leaders that I have served with. I am forever grateful for his example of leadership and mentorship.

Finally, my children who motivated me daily even now, to be the best example and version of myself because they deserved my very best; and now they are paying it forward.

About the Author

Isaiah (Ike) Johnson has a lifetime of service and a proven history of innovative leadership. Born in rural Mississippi, Ike's early years taught him Character and the values of hard work, looking out for one's neighbors, and giving back to the community. These early lessons set him on a path of service to his country and community that guides his steps today. Ike Johnson is a community resource.

In 1972, Ike enlisted in the United States Marine Corps, beginning a career that would span twenty-seven years. He earned the ranks of Private through Gunnery Sergeant, Warrant Officer One and Two, and then Limited Duty Officer, First Lieutenant to Major. After twenty-seven years of service, Ike Johnson retired at the rank of Major. He is a Desert Strom Combat Veteran who earned a Bronze Star during combat. He's also a Corporate Executive who managed thirty-two Food Service Marine Corps mess halls and led employees throughout the East Coast.

As a dedicated family man serving in the Marine Corps, Ike earned two Bachelor of Arts degrees (Psychology and Criminal Justice) and a Master of Science Degree in Human Resource Management. He is married to Annette Johnson, and they have two children.

Isaiah Ike Johnson. Published the book; "From Average to Excellent: How I Transformed My Dreams into Goals, Goals Into Plans, and Plans Into Success."

Table of Contents

1

The Essence of Visionary Leadership

Visionary leadership is a style of leadership that involves having a clear and compelling vision for the future of an organization and inspiring others to work towards achieving that vision. A visionary leader possesses the ability to anticipate and imagine future possibilities, set ambitious goals, and motivate and guide their team towards realizing those goals. The impact of visionary leadership on organizations can be significant.

Here are some key points:

Inspires and Motivates:

A visionary leader inspires and motivates their team by painting a compelling picture of the future. They communicate their vision with passion and enthusiasm, igniting a sense of purpose and commitment among employees.

This inspiration can drive individuals to go above and beyond their normal capabilities, fostering innovation and creativity within the organization.

Sets a Clear Direction:

Visionary leaders provide a clear direction for the organization. They define the purpose, values, and goals that guide decision-making and actions. This clarity helps align the efforts of individuals towards a common vision, reducing ambiguity and promoting unity among team members.

Encourages Strategic Thinking:

Visionary leaders will encourage strategic thinking among their team members. They promote a forward-thinking mindset, challenging the status quo and encouraging individuals to think beyond immediate challenges. This mindset fosters a culture of innovation and adaptability, enabling organizations to stay ahead of the competition and navigate change effectively.

Fosters Organizational Growth and Development:

Through their vision, visionary leaders drive organizational growth and development. They identify new opportunities, trends, and markets and guide the organization to pursue them.

By constantly pushing boundaries and seeking improvement, visionary leaders help organizations stay relevant and achieve long-term success.

Builds trust and Loyalty:

Visionary leaders build trust and loyalty among their team members. Their ability to articulate a compelling vision and lead by example creates a sense of trust and confidence in their leadership. Employees are more likely to stay committed and engaged when they believe in the vision and trust the leader's ability to guide the organization toward it.

Enhances Organizational Culture:

Visionary leaders play a significant role in shaping the organizational culture. They set the tone for innovation, collaboration, and continuous improvement. Their vision creates a sense of purpose and identity, attracting like-minded individuals who align with the organization's values and goals. This strong culture fosters a positive work environment, employee satisfaction, and organizational success.

****

In summary, visionary leadership has a profound impact on organizations by inspiring and motivating employees, setting a clear direction, encouraging strategic thinking, fostering growth and development, building trust and loyalty, and enhancing organizational culture. It enables organizations to adapt to change, seize opportunities, and achieve long-term success.

Visionary leaders possess certain characteristics and qualities that set them apart. Here are some key traits of visionary leaders:

Strong Vision:

Visionary leaders have a clear and compelling vision for the future. They can see beyond the present challenges and envision what they could be. This vision serves as a guiding force for the organization and inspires others to work towards its realization.

Creativity and Innovation:

Visionary leaders are creative thinkers who embrace innovation. They constantly seek new ideas, approaches, and solutions to drive progress and stay ahead of the competition. They encourage a culture of creativity and experimentation within the organization.

Strategic Thinking:

Visionary leaders possess critical thinking skills. They can analyze complex situations, anticipate trends and changes, and make informed decisions that align with the organization's vision. They can see the bigger picture and make long-term plans.

Excellent Communication:

Visionary leaders need to be exceptional communicators. They can articulate their vision in a compelling and inspiring manner, effectively conveying their ideas to others. They listen actively, encourage open dialogue, and ensure that everyone understands and embraces the vision.

Passion and Enthusiasm:

Visionary leaders are passionate about their vision and the work they do. Their energy and enthusiasm are contagious, motivating and inspiring others to share their passion. They lead by example, showing dedication and commitment to the vision.

Empathy and Emotional Intelligence:

Visionary leaders understand the importance of empathy and emotional intelligence. They can connect with others on an emotional level, understanding their needs, concerns, and motivations. They foster a supportive and inclusive environment where everyone feels valued and heard.

Risk-Taking and Resilience:

Visionary leaders are willing to take calculated risks in pursuit of their vision. They understand that growth and progress often come with uncertainty and challenges. They are resilient, able to bounce back from setbacks and learn from failures.

Collaboration and Empowerment:

They understand the power of collaboration and teamwork. They empower others to contribute their ideas and talents, fostering a sense of ownership and accountability. They build strong relationships and partnerships both within and outside the organization.

Lifelong Learning:

Visionary leaders have a thirst for knowledge and a commitment to continuous learning. They stay updated on industry trends, seek feedback and insights, and invest in their own personal and professional growth. They encourage a learning culture within the organization.

Ethical and Values-Driven:

Visionary leaders operate with integrity and uphold strong ethical standards. They are guided by a set of core values and principles that shape their decision-making and actions. They prioritize the well-being of their employees and stakeholders.

These characteristics and qualities enable visionary leaders to inspire, motivate, and lead organizations toward success by turning their vision into reality.

****

Vision plays a crucial role in setting a clear direction and inspiring others in several ways:

Provides a Sense of Purpose:

A clear vision provides a sense of purpose and direction to individuals and organizations. It answers the fundamental question of "why" and gives meaning to the work being done. When people understand the purpose behind their actions, they are more motivated and committed.

Guided Decision-Making:

A vision serves as a guiding framework for decision-making. It helps leaders and team members make choices and prioritize actions that are aligned with the desired future. When everyone is working towards a common vision, decision-making becomes more focused and consistent.

Inspires and Motivates:

A compelling vision has the power to inspire and motivate others. It sparks enthusiasm and energy, creating a shared sense of excitement and commitment. People are more likely to give their best when they can see the bigger picture and feel inspired by a compelling vision.

Fosters Innovation and Creativity:

A vision encourages innovation and creativity. When people have a clear vision in mind, they are more likely to think outside the box, explore new ideas, and take risks. A vision that embraces innovation inspires individuals to challenge the status quo and find new ways of doing things.

Builds a Shared Culture:

A vision helps build a shared culture within an organization. It sets the tone for the values, beliefs, and behaviors that are encouraged and rewarded. When everyone is aligned around a common vision, it creates a sense of belonging and unity, leading to a stronger organizational culture.

Attracts and Retains Talent:

A compelling vision acts as a magnet for talent. It attracts individuals who are aligned with the vision and share the same values and aspirations. People want to be part of something meaningful and impactful. A clear vision helps in attracting and retaining top talent.

Enhances Focus and Productivity:

Vision provides clarity and focus. It helps individuals and teams prioritize their efforts and avoid distractions. When people have a clear direction, they can channel their energy and resources toward achieving the vision, leading to increased productivity and efficiency.

Encourages Collaboration and Teamwork:

A shared vision encourages collaboration and teamwork. When everyone is working towards a common goal, it fosters a sense of collective responsibility and collaboration. Individuals are more willing to work together, share ideas, and support each other in achieving the vision.

****

Vision plays a vital role in setting a clear direction and inspiring others. It provides a purpose, guides decision-making, inspires motivation, fosters innovation, builds culture, attracts talent, enhances focus, and encourages collaboration. A compelling vision is a powerful tool that drives individuals and organizations toward success.

2

Crafting a Compelling Vision

A compelling vision is composed of several key components that make it inspiring and impactful. These components include:

Clear and Concise:

A compelling vision is clear, concise, and easily understood by everyone. It should communicate the desired outcome or future state in a simple and straightforward manner. Clarity ensures that everyone is on the same page and can easily connect with the vision.

Inspiring and Aspirational:

A compelling vision should inspire and motivate people. It should paint a vivid picture of a desirable future that goes beyond the current reality. An aspirational vision challenges individuals to reach their full potential and create something meaningful and impactful.

Challenging Yet Achievable:

A compelling vision strikes the right balance between being challenging and achievable. It should stretch individuals and organizations to push their limits and go beyond their comfort zones. At the same time, it should be realistic and attainable with the right effort and resources.

Aligned with Values and Purpose:

A compelling vision is aligned with the values and purpose of individuals and organizations. It should reflect the core beliefs and principles that guide actions and decision-making. When the vision aligns with values and purpose, it creates a sense of authenticity and commitment.

Future-Oriented:

A compelling vision focuses on the future rather than the present. It looks ahead and envisions a better tomorrow. By focusing on the future, the vision encourages individuals to think long-term and plan for sustainable growth and success.

Inclusive and Collaborative:

A compelling vision involves and engages everyone. It should be inclusive, allowing individuals to see themselves as part of the vision and contribute to its realization. Collaboration is key, as it brings together diverse perspectives and harnesses the collective wisdom and creativity of the team.

Measurable and Time-Bound:

A compelling vision includes measurable goals and a timeline for achievement. It provides a sense of progress and allows individuals and organizations to track their success. Setting specific milestones and deadlines adds a sense of urgency and accountability to the vision.

Communicated Effectively:

A compelling vision needs to be communicated effectively to ensure understanding and buy-in. It should be shared through various channels and repeated consistently. Communication should be clear, passionate, and tailored to the needs and preferences of the audience.

By incorporating these components, a compelling vision becomes a powerful tool for setting a clear direction and inspiring others. It provides a roadmap for success and rallies individuals and organizations around a common purpose.

****

Developing a vision statement that truly resonates with people requires careful thought and consideration.

Here are some techniques to help you create a compelling vision statement:

Reflect on your Values and Purpose:

Start by understanding your core values and the purpose of your organization. Consider what drives you and what you hope to achieve in the long term. Your vision statement should align with these values and purpose to create a sense of authenticity and passion.

Involve Key Stakeholders:

Engage key stakeholders, such as employees, customers, and partners, in the process of developing the vision statement. Seek their input and perspectives to ensure that the vision resonates with those who will be impacted by it. This collaborative approach fosters a sense of ownership and commitment.

Use Inspiring and Emotive Language:

Choose words that evoke emotion and inspiration. Use language that paints a vivid picture of the desired future and connects people on an emotional level. This helps create a sense of excitement and motivation around the vision.

Be Concise and Focused:

Keep your vision statement concise and focused. Avoid using jargon or complex language that may confuse or alienate people. A clear and simple vision statement is easier to remember and communicate.

Make it aspirational and ambitious:

Your vision statement should be aspirational and push the boundaries of what is currently possible. It should challenge people to think big and strive for greatness. Aim for a vision that inspires and motivates individuals to go above and beyond.

Ensure it is Realistic and Achievable:

While it's important to have an ambitious vision, it should also be realistic and achievable. Consider the resources, capabilities, and constraints of your organization. A vision that seems too far-fetched or unattainable may discourage people instead of motivating them.

Test and Iterate:

Share your vision statement with a diverse group of individuals and gather feedback. Pay attention to their reactions and suggestions. Use this feedback to refine and improve your vision statement. Iteration is key to developing a vision statement that truly resonates.

Communicate Effectively:

Once you have developed your vision statement, communicate it effectively across your organization and beyond. Use various communication channels, such as company meetings, newsletters, and intranets, to ensure that everyone is aware of and understands the vision. Reinforce the vision consistently to keep it at the top of your mind.

Remember, a compelling vision statement should inspire, motivate, and resonate with people. It should capture the essence of what you aspire to achieve and create a shared sense of purpose and direction.

****

Aligning the vision with organizational values and goals is crucial for creating a vision statement that resonates with stakeholders and guides the direction of the organization.

Here are some steps to align your vision with your values and goals:

Identify your Core Values:

Start by identifying the core values that define your organization. These values represent the fundamental beliefs and principles that guide decision-making and behavior. Ensure that your vision statement reflects and upholds these values.

Define your Organizational Goals:

Clarify the specific goals and objectives that your organization aims to achieve. These goals should be aligned with your values and contribute to the overall vision. Consider both short-term and long-term goals to provide a clear direction for the organization.

Connect Values and Goals to the Vision:

Examine how your values and goals align with the desired future outlined in your vision statement. Identify the common threads and connections between them. Your vision should serve as a guiding star that reflects your values and guides the pursuit of your goals.

Ensure Consistency and Coherence:

Evaluate the consistency and coherence between your vision, values, and goals. Make sure that they complement and reinforce each other. If there are any inconsistencies, adjust your vision or goals to ensure alignment.

Involve Stakeholders:

Engage key stakeholders, such as employees, customers, and partners, in the process of aligning your vision with values and goals. Seek their input and feedback to ensure that the vision resonates with them and reflects their perspectives. This collaborative approach fosters a sense of ownership and commitment.

Communicate the Alignment:

Clearly communicate how your vision aligns with your organizational values and goals. Share this information with your stakeholders through various communication channels, such as company-wide meetings, internal newsletters, and employee training sessions. Reinforce the connection between vision, values, and goals to create a shared understanding and commitment.

Review and Update Regularly:

Regularly review and update your vision, values, and goals to ensure they remain relevant and aligned with the changing needs and dynamics of your organization. As your organization evolves, you may need to adjust and maintain alignment.

****

By aligning your vision with your organizational values and goals, you create a powerful framework that guides decision-making, shapes organizational culture, and inspires action. It establishes a clear sense of purpose and direction, leading to a greater sense of cohesion and motivation among stakeholders.

3

Communicating Vision

Communicating the vision effectively to stakeholders is crucial for gaining their support and buy-in.

Here are some strategies to help you effectively communicate your vision:

Clearly Articulate the Vision:

Start by clearly articulating the vision in a concise and compelling manner. Use language that is easy to understand and resonates with stakeholders. Avoid jargon or technical terms that may confuse or alienate them. Paint a vivid picture of the desired future state that the vision represents.

Use Storytelling:

Use storytelling techniques to bring the vision to life. Share stories, anecdotes, or examples that illustrate how the vision will positively impact the organization and its stakeholders. Storytelling helps to create an emotional connection and make the vision more tangible and relatable.

Tailor the Message to Different Stakeholders:

Consider the needs, interests, and concerns of different stakeholder groups. Tailor your message to address their specific perspectives and how the vision will impact them directly. Highlight the benefits and opportunities that the vision brings to each stakeholder group.

Provide Context and Rationale:

Explain the context and rationale behind the vision to help stakeholders understand. Explain the reasons why the vision is important and how it aligns with the organization's values and goals. Share any market trends, industry changes, or internal factors that influenced the development of the vision.

Engage in Two-Way Communication: F

Foster a culture of open communication by encouraging feedback and questions from stakeholders. Create opportunities for dialogue and discussion about the vision. Listen actively to their concerns, ideas, and suggestions. This two-way communication builds trust and allows stakeholders to feel heard and valued.

Use Visual Aid:

Utilize visual aids such as presentations, infographics, or videos to improve engagement. Visuals can help stakeholders better understand and remember the key messages. Use imagery, graphs, or diagrams to illustrate the current state, the desired future state, and the path to get there.

Demonstrate Leadership Commitment:

Show your own commitment to the vision by leading by example. Be passionate and enthusiastic when discussing the vision with stakeholders. Demonstrate how the vision guides your decision-making and actions. When stakeholders see your dedication, they are more likely to believe in and support the vision.

Repeat and Reinforce the Message:

Consistently reinforce the vision message through various communication channels and platforms. Repeat the key messages and remind stakeholders of the vision regularly. Use multiple touchpoints, such as team meetings, newsletters, emails, and social media, to ensure the message reaches all stakeholders.

Celebrate Milestones and Successes:

Celebrate and recognize achievements that align with the vision. Highlight success stories and milestones along the way. This reinforces the progress being made toward the vision and motivates stakeholders to continue supporting their realization.

Monitor Feedback and Adapt:

Continuously monitor stakeholder feedback and adapt your communication strategies accordingly. Stay open to suggestions and ideas for improvement. Adjust your communication approach to address any concerns or misconceptions that arise.

By employing these strategies, you can effectively communicate your vision to stakeholders, inspire their support, and create a shared sense of purpose and commitment toward achieving the vision.

****

Building a shared sense of purpose and commitment among stakeholders is essential for driving alignment and achieving organizational goals.

Here are some strategies to help you foster a shared sense of purpose and commitment:

Clearly Define and Communicate the Organizational Purpose:

Start by clearly defining the purpose of your organization. Articulate the "why" behind what you do and how it positively impacts society or the community. Communicate with this purpose consistently and ensure that it resonates with all stakeholders.

Involve Stakeholders in Goal Setting:

Involve stakeholders in the goal-setting process to ensure their perspectives and input are considered. This creates a sense of ownership and commitment towards the shared goals. Collaboratively establish goals that align with the organization's purpose and values.

Connect Individual Roles to the Bigger Picture:

Help stakeholders understand how their individual roles contribute to the overall organizational purpose. Clearly communicate the impact and importance of each role in achieving the shared goals. Show how their contributions directly support the organization's mission.

Foster Open and Transparent Communication:

Create an environment of open and transparent communication where all stakeholders feel comfortable expressing their thoughts, ideas, and concerns. Encourage regular dialogue and provide opportunities for feedback. This helps build trust and strengthens the sense of shared purpose.

Celebrate Achievements and Milestones:

Regularly acknowledge and celebrate individual and collective achievements that contribute to the shared goals. Recognize the efforts and successes of stakeholders, highlighting how they are moving closer to the shared purpose. This reinforces commitment and motivates further engagement.

Provide Opportunities for Growth and Development:

Offer opportunities for stakeholders to enhance their skills, knowledge, and capabilities. Invest in their professional development and provide resources for continuous learning. When stakeholders feel supported and empowered, they are more likely to be committed to the shared purpose.

Lead by Example:

Demonstrate your own commitment to the shared purpose through your actions and decisions. Model the behaviors and values that align with the purpose. Be consistent in your communication and demonstrate integrity and authenticity. When stakeholders see leaders living the shared purpose, they are more likely to follow suit.

Foster Collaboration and Teamwork:

Encourage collaboration and teamwork among stakeholders. Create cross-functional teams and projects that bring together individuals from different areas of the organization. This promotes a sense of collective ownership and fosters a collaborative culture centered around a shared purpose.

Seek Input and Involve Stakeholders in Decision-Making:

Involve stakeholders in decision-making processes that impact the shared purpose. Seek their input, listen to their perspectives, and consider their ideas. When stakeholders feel their voices are heard and valued, they are more likely to be committed to the shared purpose.

Continuously Communicate and Reinforce the Shared Purpose:

Regularly communicate and reinforce the shared purpose through various channels and platforms. Use different communication methods such as town hall meetings, newsletters, intranets, and social media to consistently remind stakeholders of the shared purpose and its importance.

By implementing these strategies, you can build a strong sense of shared purpose and commitment among stakeholders. This shared purpose will drive alignment, engagement, and collaboration towards achieving the organization's goals.

****

Overcoming resistance and fostering buy-in is crucial when implementing new initiatives or changes within an organization. Here are some strategies to help you navigate resistance and gain buy-in from stakeholders:

Communicate the "Why:"

Clearly communicate the reasons behind the proposed change or initiative. Explain the benefits and the impact it will have on the organization, teams, and individuals. Help stakeholders understand the need for change and how it aligns with the organization's goals and values.

Address Concerns and Listen Actively:

Take the time to listen to the concerns and objections of stakeholders. Give them a platform to express their thoughts and feelings about the proposed change. Address their concerns empathetically and provide transparent and honest answers. Showing that you value their input and are willing to address their concerns can help build trust and reduce resistance.

Create a Sense of Ownership:

Involve stakeholders in the decision-making process as much as possible. Seek their input and feedback and consider their perspectives when shaping the change. When stakeholders feel like they have a voice and are part of the process, they are more likely to take ownership of the change and support its implementation.

Highlight the Benefits and Value:

Clearly communicate the benefits and value that the change will bring. Show stakeholders how the change will improve processes, increase efficiency, or enhance outcomes. Help them envision a positive future state and the opportunities that the change will create. By emphasizing the benefits, you can generate enthusiasm and build buy-ins.

Provide Information and Resources:

Ensure that stakeholders have access to the necessary information and resources to understand and adapt to the change. Offer training, workshops, or resources to help them develop the skills and knowledge required. The more equipped stakeholders feel, the more likely they are to embrace the change and support its implementation.

Create a Culture of Open Communication:

Foster an environment where open communication is encouraged and valued. Create opportunities for dialogue, feedback, and discussion. Encourage stakeholders to express their opinions and ideas openly. This helps to build trust, encourage collaboration, and reduce resistance.

Lead by Example:

Demonstrate your own commitment to the change by leading by example. Embrace the change yourself and show enthusiasm and dedication. Your actions and behaviors will influence how others perceive and respond to the change. When stakeholders see your commitment, they are more likely to follow suit.

Foster Collaboration and Teamwork:

Leaders should encourage collaboration and teamwork among stakeholders during the change process. Create cross-functional teams or working groups to facilitate cooperation and collective problem-solving. By involving stakeholders in collaborative efforts, you can foster a sense of ownership and build a buy-in.

Celebrate Small Wins:

Acknowledge and celebrate small wins along the way. Recognize and appreciate the efforts and progress made by stakeholders during the change process. Celebrating milestones and achievements helps to keep morale high and motivates stakeholders to continue supporting the change.

Provide Ongoing Support and Feedback:

Offer ongoing support to stakeholders as they adapt to the change. Provide feedback and guidance to help them navigate any challenges or uncertainties. Regularly check in with stakeholders to address any issues or concerns that arise. By providing continuous support, you can help stakeholders overcome resistance and foster buy-in.

****

Remember that overcoming resistance and fostering buy-in is an ongoing process. It requires clear communication, active listening, empathy, and continuous engagement with stakeholders. By implementing these strategies, you can increase the likelihood of successful change implementation and gain the support of your stakeholders.

4

Inspiring and Motivating Others

Creating a culture of innovation and creativity within an organization is essential for staying competitive and driving continuous growth. Here are some strategies to help foster such a culture:

Encourage and Reward Curiosity:

Encourage employees to ask questions, explore new ideas, and challenge the status quo. Create an environment where curiosity is celebrated and rewarded. Recognize and appreciate individuals who actively seek knowledge and are open to learning.

Provide Autonomy and Freedom:

Give employees the freedom to experiment, take risks, and make decisions. Empower them to explore new approaches and solutions to problems. By providing autonomy, you encourage innovation and creativity, as individuals feel trusted and empowered to think outside the box.

Foster Collaboration and Diversity:

Visionary leaders should encourage collaboration and create opportunities for cross-functional teams to work together. Embrace diversity, as diverse perspectives and experiences can lead to innovative ideas. Create platforms for employees to share their insights, collaborate on projects, and learn from one another.

Promote a Learning Mindset:

Cultivate a culture of continuous learning and improvement. Encourage employees to develop new skills, attend training programs, and share their knowledge with others. Create a supportive environment where mistakes are seen as learning opportunities and experimentation is encouraged.

Provide Resources and Tools:

Ensure that employees have access to the necessary resources, tools, and technology to support their innovative efforts. Provide training and workshops on creativity techniques and problem-solving methods. Invest in research and development to stay at the forefront of innovation.

Lead by Example:

Leaders play a crucial role in shaping the culture of an organization. Lead by example by embracing innovation and creativity yourself. Demonstrate a willingness to try new things, take calculated risks, and learn from failures. Your actions will inspire and motivate others to follow suit.

Celebrate and Recognize Innovation:

Celebrate and recognize individuals and teams who demonstrate innovative thinking and contribute to the organization's growth. Implement recognition programs, innovation challenges, or idea-sharing platforms to highlight and reward creative contributions.

Encourage Cross-Pollination of Ideas:

Create opportunities for employees from different departments or teams to interact with and exchange ideas. Foster a culture of knowledge sharing and collaboration across the organization. Encourage employees to attend conferences, participate in industry events, or engage in external networks to gain fresh perspectives.

Create a Safe Space for Experimentation:

Encourage employees to experiment and try new ideas without fear of failure or judgment. Foster a culture where mistakes are seen as stepping stones to success and where individuals are encouraged to learn from their failures. Provide support and guidance to help employees learn from their experiences and iterate their ideas.

Continuously Communicate the Importance of Innovation:

Regularly communicate the importance of innovation and creativity to all employees. Help them understand how their contributions can make a difference and drive the organization forward. Share success stories and case studies to inspire and motivate employees to think innovatively.

Remember that creating a culture of innovation and creativity is an ongoing effort. It requires consistent support, encouragement, and reinforcement from leaders and managers. By implementing these strategies, you can foster an environment where innovation and creativity thrive, leading to new ideas, improved processes, and a competitive advantage for your organization.

****

Empowering individuals to take ownership of the vision is crucial for driving success and fostering a culture of innovation and creativity. Here are some strategies to help empower individuals in this way:

Clearly Communicate the Vision:

Ensure that the vision of the organization is clearly defined and communicated to all employees. Make sure they understand the purpose, values, and long-term goals of the organization. A clear vision provides a sense of direction and purpose, enabling individuals to align their efforts and take ownership.

Encourage Autonomy and Decision-Making:

Give individuals the freedom to make decisions and take ownership of their work. Provide them with the necessary resources, support, and guidance, and then step back and allow them to take the lead. Empowerment comes from trusting individuals to make informed decisions and giving them the autonomy to execute their ideas.

Delegate Responsibility and Authority:

Delegate meaningful tasks and responsibilities to individuals, allowing them to take ownership of specific projects or initiatives. By giving them authority over their work, you enable them to take ownership and make a direct impact on the organization's success. Regularly check in to provide guidance and support, but avoid micromanaging.

Foster a Culture of Accountability:

Establish a culture where individuals are accountable for their actions and outcomes. Encourage individuals to set clear goals and objectives and regularly review progress. Celebrate successes and address challenges collectively. When individuals feel accountable for their work, they are more likely to take ownership and strive for excellence.

Provide Opportunities for Growth and Development:

Invest in the growth and development of individuals by offering training, mentorship programs, and opportunities for learning. Help individuals develop the skills and knowledge needed to take ownership of their work and contribute to the vision. Encourage them to seek out new challenges and take on stretch assignments.

Recognize and Reward Initiative:

Acknowledge and appreciate individuals who take initiative and demonstrate ownership of the vision. Celebrate their accomplishments and recognize their contributions. This recognition can take the form of public praise, rewards, promotions, or increased responsibilities. Recognizing and rewarding ownership reinforces the desired behavior and motivates others to follow suit.

Encourage Collaboration and Teamwork:

Foster a collaborative environment where individuals can work together to achieve the vision. Encourage cross-functional collaboration and create opportunities for individuals to contribute their unique perspectives and skills. By working collaboratively, individuals can leverage their strengths and collectively take ownership of the vision.

Lead by Example:

As a leader, it is essential to lead by example and demonstrate ownership of the vision yourself. Show enthusiasm, passion, and commitment to the organization's goals. Model the desired behavior and showcase how taking ownership can drive success. When individuals see leaders taking ownership, they are more likely to do the same.

Provide Regular Feedback and Support:

Offer regular feedback and support to individuals as they take ownership of the vision. Provide constructive feedback to help them grow and improve.

Be available to answer questions, provide guidance, and offer resources. Creating a supportive environment encourages individuals to take ownership and fosters their development.

Celebrate and Share Success Stories:

Celebrate and share success stories of individuals who have taken ownership of the vision and made a significant impact. Highlight their achievements and the positive outcomes they have driven. These success stories serve as inspiration and demonstrate the value of ownership to others in the organization.

By implementing these strategies, you can empower individuals to take ownership of the vision, fostering a culture of innovation, creativity, and accountability. When individuals feel empowered and take ownership, they are more likely to go above and beyond, contribute their best work, and drive the organization towards its goals.

****

Recognizing and rewarding contributions to the vision is essential for motivating individuals, reinforcing desired behaviors, and fostering a culture of ownership and excellence.

Here are some strategies to effectively recognize and reward contributions to the vision:

Public Recognition:

Publicly acknowledge and appreciate individuals' contributions during team meetings, company-wide announcements, or newsletters. Highlight specific actions, projects, or initiatives that align with the vision and have made a significant impact. This public recognition not only rewards the individual but also inspires others to follow suit.

Personalized Feedback:

Provide individuals with specific and timely feedback on their contributions to the vision. Recognize their efforts, highlight the positive outcomes they have achieved, and express gratitude for their commitment. Personalized feedback shows that their work is valued and encourages them to continue making meaningful contributions.

Performance-based Incentives:

Consider implementing performance-based incentives such as bonuses, promotions, or salary increases tied to individuals' contributions to the vision. Reward those who consistently demonstrate ownership, go above and beyond, and drive the organization closer to its long-term goals. These incentives provide tangible recognition and motivate individuals to continually strive for excellence.

Opportunities for Growth and Development:

Offer individuals opportunities for professional growth and development as a reward for their contributions. This can include access to specialized training, conferences, workshops, or mentorship programs. By investing in their growth, you not only recognize their efforts but also empower them to further contribute to the vision.

Employee of the Month/Quarter/Year:

Implement an employee recognition program where outstanding individuals are selected as "Employee of the Month," "Quarter," or "Year" based on their contributions to the vision. These types of programs acknowledge exceptional performance, encourage healthy competition, and boost morale within the organization.

Team Celebrations and Rewards:

Organize team celebrations or outings to commemorate milestones achieved through collective effort towards the vision. This can include team launches, offsite activities, or recognition events. By celebrating as a team, you reinforce the importance of collaboration and recognize the collective contributions towards the vision.

Opportunities for Increased Responsibility:

Reward individuals who consistently demonstrate ownership and make significant contributions by offering them increased responsibility. This can involve leading a new project, heading a team, or representing the organization in external initiatives. Increased responsibility serves as both a recognition and a growth opportunity for individuals.

Encourage Peer Recognition:

Foster a culture of peer recognition by encouraging team members to acknowledge and appreciate each other's contributions. This can be through a formal peer recognition program, where individuals nominate and recognize their colleagues for their outstanding work. Peer recognition creates a supportive and collaborative environment and reinforces the value of contributions to the vision.

Personalized Rewards and Incentives:

Consider offering personalized rewards or incentives based on an individual's preferences and interests. This could include gift cards, extra time off, or special privileges. Tailoring rewards to individuals' preferences shows that their contributions are valued at a personal level, further motivating them to continue their efforts.

Continuous Feedback and Support:

Provide ongoing feedback and support to individuals as they contribute to the vision. Regularly check in, offer guidance, and provide resources to help them succeed. Recognize their progress and offer constructive feedback to encourage further growth and improvement.

****

Remember, effective recognition and rewards should be meaningful, timely, and aligned with the organization's values and goals. By implementing these strategies, you can create a culture where individuals feel valued, motivated, and empowered to contribute their best work towards the vision.

5

Leading Change and Adaptation

Embracing change as a catalyst for growth and progress is crucial in today's dynamic and fast-paced world. Change presents opportunities for innovation, learning, and improvement.

Here are some ways to embrace change and harness its power for personal and organizational growth:

Cultivate a Growth Mindset:

Adopt a mindset that sees change as an opportunity for growth and learning. Embrace the belief that challenges and setbacks are valuable experiences that can lead to new insights and skills. Encourage yourself and others to view change as a chance to expand capabilities and explore new possibilities.

Foster a Culture of Continuous Learning:

Create an environment where learning and development are valued and encouraged. Provide resources, training programs, and opportunities for employees to acquire new knowledge and skills.

Encourage individuals to seek feedback and reflect on their experiences to promote continuous improvement.

Encourage Open Communication:

Create channels for open and transparent communication to foster a culture where ideas, concerns, and suggestions are freely shared. Encourage individuals to voice their opinions and perspectives on changes happening within the organization. This promotes dialogue, collaboration, and a sense of ownership in the change process.

Emphasize Adaptability and Resilience:

Develop the ability to adapt to change and bounce back from challenges. Encourage individuals to be flexible, open-minded, and willing to explore new approaches. Provide support and resources to help individuals navigate and overcome obstacles that may arise during the change process.

Lead by Example:

As a leader, demonstrate a positive attitude towards change and be an advocate for embracing it. Show enthusiasm, curiosity, and a willingness to learn and adapt. Lead by example in embracing change and inspire others to do the same.

Encourage Experimentation and Innovation:

Create a safe space for individuals to experiment and take calculated risks. Encourage creativity and innovation by empowering individuals to explore new ideas and approaches. Recognize and reward innovative thinking and solutions that arise from embracing change.

Provide Clarity and Purpose:

Clearly communicate the reasons behind the change and the vision for the future. Help individuals understand how their roles and contributions fit into the bigger picture. Providing a sense of purpose and direction helps individuals see change as a necessary step toward progress and growth.

Celebrate Successes and Milestones:

Acknowledge and celebrate achievements and milestones that result from embracing change. Recognize and appreciate the efforts and contributions of individuals and teams. Celebrating successes reinforces the positive impact of change and motivates individuals to continue embracing it.

Encourage Collaboration and Teamwork:

Foster a collaborative environment where individuals can work together to navigate change. Promote cross-functional collaboration and encourage knowledge-sharing. By working together, individuals can leverage each other's strengths and experiences to effectively adapt and grow.

Reflect and Learn from Experiences:

Encourage individuals and teams to reflect on the outcomes and lessons learned from the changing process. Facilitate discussions to identify areas of improvement and opportunities for further growth. Encourage a continuous improvement mindset and apply insights gained from past experiences to future endeavors.

****

By embracing change as a catalyst for growth and progress, individuals and organizations can stay agile, innovative, and resilient in the face of evolving circumstances. It is through embracing change that we can uncover new possibilities, drive positive transformation, and achieve long-term success. Managing resistance and navigating challenges are essential skills when embracing change.

Here are some strategies to help you effectively address resistance and overcome challenges:

Communicate Openly and Transparently:

Clearly communicate the reasons behind the change, the expected benefits, and the impact on individuals and the organization. Address concerns and provide regular updates to keep everyone informed. Open and transparent communication helps build trust and reduces resistance.

Involve Stakeholders Early On:

Involve key stakeholders in the change process from the beginning. Seek their input, listen to their concerns, and involve them in decision-making. By involving stakeholders, you create a sense of ownership and increase their commitment to the change.

Empathize and Address Concerns:

Understand that resistance to change often stems from fear, uncertainty, or perceived loss. Empathize with individuals' concerns and address them openly. Provide opportunities for individuals to express their thoughts and concerns and actively listen and respond with empathy.

Provide Support and Resources:

Offer support and resources to help individuals navigate the change. Provide training, coaching, or mentoring to equip individuals with the necessary skills and knowledge. Be responsive to individual needs and aid when needed.

Break down the change into Manageable Steps:

Complex changes can be overwhelming, leading to resistance. Break down the change into smaller, manageable steps or milestones. This makes the change process more approachable and allows individuals to see progress, boosting their confidence and motivation.

Foster a Culture of Collaboration:

Encourage collaboration and teamwork during the change process. Create opportunities for individuals to work together, share ideas, and problem-solve. Collaboration helps build a sense of support and collective ownership, reducing resistance and increasing engagement.

Celebrate Small Wins:

Acknowledge and celebrate small victories along the way. Recognize and appreciate the efforts and achievements of individuals and teams. Celebrating milestones boosts morale, encourages continued progress, and helps overcome challenges.

Anticipate and Address Obstacles:

Proactively identify potential obstacles and develop strategies to address them. Anticipate resistance points and challenges that may arise during the change process. Having contingency plans in place helps minimize disruptions and keeps the change process on track.

Seek Feedback and Learn from Experiences:

Regularly seek feedback from individuals and teams involved in the change process. Encourage open and honest feedback to identify areas of improvement and address concerns. Reflect on the experiences and lessons learned and apply those insights to future change initiatives.

Lead by Example:

As a leader, demonstrate a positive attitude towards change and resilience in the face of challenges. Actively participate in the change process and model the desired behaviors. Your actions and attitude influence others and can help overcome resistance and navigate challenges more effectively.

****

Remember, change can be challenging, and resistance is a natural part of the process. By implementing these strategies, you can effectively manage resistance, navigate challenges, and create a supportive environment for embracing change and achieving growth and progress. Building resilience and agility is crucial in navigating uncertain and challenging situations.

Here are some strategies to help you develop resilience and agility:

Cultivate a Growth Mindset:

Embrace a mindset that views challenges as opportunities for growth and learning. Instead of focusing on what cannot be controlled, concentrate on what you can do to adapt and overcome. See setbacks as temporary and believe in your ability to bounce back.

Develop Self-Awareness:

Understand your strengths, weaknesses, and triggers. Self-awareness allows you to recognize your emotions, thoughts, and reactions in uncertain situations. By being aware of your own patterns, you can better manage them and make conscious choices.

Practice mindfulness and stress management:

Engage in mindfulness techniques such as deep breathing, meditation, or journaling. These practices help reduce stress and increase self-awareness. Regular exercise, proper sleep, and a healthy diet also contribute to overall well-being and resilience.

Build a Support Network:

Surround yourself with a supportive network of friends, family, mentors, or colleagues who can provide guidance, encouragement, and perspective. Lean on these relationships during challenging times, and be open to seeking help when needed.

Foster Adaptability:

Embrace change and uncertainty as opportunities for growth. Develop flexibility and adaptability by being open to new ideas and approaches. Practice stepping outside of your comfort zone and challenging your own assumptions and beliefs.

Focus on Problem-Solving and Solutions:

Instead of dwelling on the problems and uncertainties, shift your focus to finding solutions. Break down complex challenges into smaller, manageable tasks and take proactive steps towards resolving them. This approach helps build confidence and agility.

Learn from Past Experiences:

Reflect on past experiences and identify lessons learned. What strategies worked, and what could have been done differently? Apply these insights to future situations, adjusting your approach as needed. This continuous learning process enhances your resilience and ability to navigate uncertainty.

Embrace a Positive Mindset:

Cultivate a positive outlook and maintain optimism, even in the face of uncertainty. Practice gratitude and focus on the things you can control and appreciate. Positivity helps to maintain resilience and find opportunities amidst challenges.

Seek New Perspectives:

Engage in diverse viewpoints and seek feedback from others. This broadens your perspective and allows you to consider alternative approaches or solutions. Being open to different opinions fosters adaptability and agility in uncertain circumstances.

Take Care of Yourself:

Prioritize self-care and well-being. Engage in activities that bring you joy and relaxation, such as hobbies, spending time in nature, or pursuing creative outlets. Taking care of yourself physically, emotionally, and mentally strengthens your resilience and ability to handle uncertainty.

****

Building resilience and agility takes time and practice. By implementing these strategies, you can develop the skills and mindset needed to thrive in the face of uncertainty and navigate challenges with greater confidence and adaptability. Remember, resilience is not about avoiding difficulties but about bouncing back stronger and more prepared than before.

6

Building High-Performing Teams

Leveraging a compelling vision can be a powerful tool for attracting and retaining top talent. Here are some strategies to effectively use your vision to attract and retain top talent:

Craft a Compelling Vision Statement:

Develop a clear and inspiring vision statement that articulates your organization's purpose, values, and long-term goals. A well-crafted vision statement creates a sense of purpose and direction, appealing to talented individuals who align with your organization's mission.

Communicate the Vision Consistently:

Regularly communicate your vision throughout the organization and to potential candidates. Use various channels such as company meetings, newsletters, social media, and the company website to share your vision and reinforce its importance. Consistent communication helps create a sense of shared purpose and attracts individuals who resonate with your vision.

Align Values and Culture:

Ensure that your organization's values and culture align with the vision you have set forth. Top talent is often attracted to organizations that share their values and offer a positive and inclusive work culture. Foster an environment that supports collaboration, innovation, and continuous learning to attract and retain high-performing individuals.

Showcase the Impact and Purpose:

Highlight the tangible impact and purpose of your organization's work. Top talent is often motivated by the opportunity to make a difference and contribute meaningfully. Share success stories, case studies, and testimonials that demonstrate the positive impact your organization has on its customers, industry, or society.

Offer Career Development Opportunities:

Top talent seeks organizations that offer growth and development opportunities. Showcase the career advancement paths within your organization and provide resources for professional development. Invest in training, mentorship programs, and opportunities for skill enhancement to attract ambitious individuals who are looking to grow and excel in their careers.

Emphasize the Employee Experience:

Create a positive employee experience that aligns with your vision. Focus on factors such as work-life balance, a supportive work environment, recognition and rewards, and opportunities for autonomy and creativity. A positive employee experience enhances employee engagement and satisfaction, making your organization an attractive place to work.

Foster a Diverse and Inclusive Workplace:

Emphasize your commitment to diversity and inclusion. Showcase initiatives and programs that promote diversity in hiring, leadership development, and decision-making processes. A diverse and inclusive workplace not only attracts top talent but also promotes innovation and creativity.

Encourage Employee Participation:

Involve employees in shaping and realizing the vision. Encourage their input, ideas, and feedback on how to achieve the vision and make it a reality. This engagement and sense of ownership create a strong bond between employees and the organization, increasing their commitment and loyalty.

Recognize and Reward Alignment with the Vision:

Acknowledge and reward employees who exemplify the values and contribute to the vision. Recognize and celebrate their achievements, both individually and collectively. This reinforces the importance of the vision and motivates employees to actively engage in its realization.

Continuously Evaluate and Refine the Vision:

Regularly assess the relevance and impact of your vision. Stay attuned to changing market dynamics, industry trends, and employee feedback. Adapt and refine the vision as needed to ensure it remains inspiring and aligned with the aspirations of top talent.

By leveraging your vision effectively, you can attract and retain top talent who are motivated by purpose, aligned with your organization's values, and committed to achieving your long-term goals. Remember, a compelling vision serves as a magnet for talented individuals and provides a strong foundation for success.

****

Fostering collaboration and synergy within teams is essential for achieving collective goals, maximizing productivity, and driving innovation.

Here are some strategies to promote collaboration and synergy within teams:

Establish Clear Goals and Shared Purpose:

Clearly define the team's goals and ensure that everyone understands and shares the purpose behind these objectives. This shared purpose creates a common focus and aligns team members toward a collective vision.

Encourage Open Communication:

Create an environment where team members feel comfortable sharing ideas, thoughts, and concerns openly. Encourage active listening and constructive feedback. This fosters a culture of trust and psychological safety, allowing for effective collaboration.

Promote Cross-Functional Collaboration:

A leader should encourage collaboration across different departments and functions within the organization. This cross-pollination of ideas and expertise can lead to innovative solutions and a broader perspective on challenges. Provide opportunities for teams to collaborate on projects or participate in cross-functional working groups.

Foster a Culture of Teamwork:

Emphasize the value of teamwork and create opportunities for team members to collaborate on tasks and projects. Recognize and reward collective achievements, reinforcing the importance of collaboration. Encourage knowledge sharing and cooperation rather than competition among team members.

Provide the Right Tools and Resources:

Ensure that teams have access to the necessary tools, technologies, and resources to collaborate effectively. This includes communication platforms, project management tools, and shared documentation systems. Use technology to facilitate virtual collaboration for remote or distributed teams.

Empower Autonomy and Ownership:

Give team members the freedom to make decisions and take ownership of their work. Encourage autonomy by providing clear expectations and guidelines while allowing individuals to use their creativity and expertise to find solutions. This empowers team members and fosters a sense of ownership and accountability.

Facilitate Team-Building Activities:

Organize team-building activities and offsite events to strengthen relationships and foster a sense of camaraderie. These activities can include team-building exercises, workshops, retreats, or social events. These activities help build trust, improve communication, and create a positive team dynamic.

Encourage Diverse Perspectives:

Embrace diversity within teams and encourage the inclusion of different perspectives and ideas. Diversity can lead to more innovative solutions and richer discussions. Create an inclusive environment where all team members feel valued and respected, regardless of their backgrounds or opinions.

Foster Learning Culture:

Promote a culture of continuous learning and growth within the team. Encourage team members to seek out new knowledge, share their expertise, and learn from each other. Provide opportunities for professional development and training to enhance skills and capabilities.

Lead by Example:

As a leader, model collaborative behavior and demonstrate the importance of teamwork. Encourage collaboration through your own actions, such as seeking input, involving team members in decision-making, and recognizing and appreciating collaborative efforts. Your leadership sets the tone for the team's collaborative culture.

****

By implementing these strategies, you can create a collaborative and synergistic team environment where individuals work together cohesively, leverage each other's strengths, and achieve outstanding results. Collaboration and synergy within teams not only enhance productivity but also contribute to a positive work culture and employee satisfaction. Developing a culture of trust, accountability, and continuous learning is crucial for fostering a positive and productive work environment.

Here are some strategies to cultivate these elements within your team:

Lead by Example:

As a leader, demonstrate trustworthiness, accountability, and a commitment to continuous learning. Model the behavior you want to see in your team members. Be transparent, admit mistakes, and take responsibility for your actions. Show a genuine desire to learn and improve.

Encourage Open and Honest Communication:

Create an environment where team members feel safe to express their thoughts, opinions, and concerns openly. Encourage active listening and provide opportunities for constructive feedback. Foster an open-door policy where team members can approach you with any issues or ideas.

Establish Clear Expectations and Goals:

Set clear expectations for performance and behavior within the team. Clearly communicate the team's goals and objectives, as well as individual responsibilities. This clarity helps build trust and ensures that everyone understands their role in achieving the team's objectives.

Foster Collaboration and Teamwork:

Encourage collaboration among team members by promoting a sense of shared purpose and collective accountability. Emphasize the importance of working together towards common goals. Provide opportunities for team members to collaborate on projects and leverage each other's strengths.

Provide Regular Feedback and Recognition:

Offer regular feedback to team members, both constructive criticism and positive reinforcement. Recognize and appreciate their contributions, which builds trust and reinforces a culture of accountability. Celebrate achievements and milestones to foster a sense of accomplishment and motivation.

Encourage Learning and Professional Development:

Support and encourage continuous learning within your team. Provide resources, such as training programs, workshops, or conferences, to enhance their skills and knowledge. Foster a growth mindset and promote the idea that learning is a lifelong journey.

Empower Decision-Making and Autonomy:

Give team members the authority to make decisions within their areas of responsibility. This fosters a sense of ownership and accountability. Encourage them to take initiative, learn from their decisions, and share what they have learned with the team.

Foster a Supportive and Inclusive Environment:

Create a culture where everyone feels valued and included. Encourage diversity of thought and perspectives. Foster a supportive atmosphere where team members feel comfortable taking risks, sharing their ideas, and expressing their opinions.

Address Conflicts and Challenges Proactively:

Address conflicts and challenges within the team in a timely and constructive manner. Encourage open dialogue to resolve issues and find mutually beneficial solutions. Provide guidance and support to help team members navigate difficult situations.

Continuously Evaluate and Improve:

Regularly assess the team's progress and performance. Collect feedback from team members and stakeholders to identify areas for improvement. Use this feedback to refine processes, address gaps, and enhance team dynamics.

****

By implementing these strategies, you can create a culture of trust, accountability, and continuous learning within your team. This positive work environment will not only enhance productivity but also foster employee engagement, satisfaction, and long-term success.

7

Leading with Integrity and Ethics

Ethical leadership plays a crucial role in visionary leadership by ensuring that the vision is pursued in a responsible and morally upright manner.

Ethical leadership is essential as it provides a moral compass and ensures that the pursuit of the vision is carried out with integrity, trust, and consideration for ethical values. By incorporating ethical principles into the vision and leading by example, visionary leaders can inspire others and create a positive and sustainable impact on their organizations and society.

Here are some reasons why ethical leadership is important in visionary leadership:

Guiding Principles:

Ethical leadership provides a set of guiding principles and values that shape the vision and direction of the organization. A visionary leader with strong ethical values ensures that the vision is aligned with the principles of honesty, integrity, fairness, and respect for others.

Trust and Credibility:

Ethical leadership builds trust and credibility among team members and stakeholders. When a leader demonstrates ethical behavior and consistently makes ethical decisions, it fosters a sense of trust and confidence in their leadership. This trust is essential for gaining the support and commitment of others towards the vision.

Stakeholder Relationships:

Ethical leadership promotes positive relationships with stakeholders, including employees, customers, investors, and the wider community. By considering the interests and well-being of all stakeholders, a visionary leader ensures that the pursuit of the vision is not at the expense of ethical considerations. This strengthens the organization's reputation and enhances its long-term sustainability.

Role Model:

Ethical leadership sets an example for others to follow. When a visionary leader consistently demonstrates ethical behavior and hold themselves accountable to high ethical standards, they inspire and motivate others to do the same. This creates a culture of ethical behavior within the organization and encourages employees to align their actions with the vision.

Decision-Making:

Visionary leaders often face complex and challenging decisions. Ethical leadership provides a framework for making ethical choices that align with the vision and values of the organization. By considering the ethical implications of their decisions, leaders can ensure that the pursuit of the vision does not compromise ethical principles.

Organizational Culture:

Ethical leadership shapes the organizational culture by promoting ethical behavior and values. A culture of ethical behavior is essential for maintaining the integrity of the vision and ensuring that it is pursued in a manner that is consistent with ethical standards. It also attracts and retains ethical employees who are aligned with the organization's values.

Social Responsibility:

Visionary leaders have a responsibility to consider the broader impact of their actions on society. Ethical leadership encourages leaders to consider the social, environmental, and ethical consequences of their decisions. By integrating social responsibility into the vision, leaders can contribute to the betterment of society while pursuing their goals.

****

Balancing the pursuit of a vision with ethical considerations is essential to ensure that the vision is achieved in a responsible and morally upright manner. Here are some strategies to achieve this balance:

Clearly Define Ethical Guidelines:

Establish clear ethical guidelines and principles that align with the organization's values and vision. Communicate these guidelines to all team members and stakeholders to ensure a shared understanding of the ethical expectations.

Involve Stakeholders in Decision-Making:

Engage key stakeholders in the decision-making process to gather diverse perspectives and insights. By considering the input of different stakeholders, including employees, customers, and community members, leaders can make more informed decisions that balance the pursuit of the vision with ethical considerations.

Conduct Ethical Impact Assessments:

Before making important decisions, assess the potential ethical impact of those decisions. Consider the potential consequences on various stakeholders, the organization's reputation, and societal implications. This assessment can help leaders identify any ethical dilemmas and find ways to mitigate potential negative impacts.

Foster a Culture of Ethical Behavior:

Create a culture that prioritizes ethical behavior and encourages employees to act in accordance with the organization's ethical guidelines. This can be achieved by promoting open communication, providing ethics training and education, and recognizing and rewarding ethical behavior.

Seek Ethical Advice and Guidance:

When faced with complex ethical dilemmas, seek advice and guidance from ethical experts or ethical committees. Engaging with external sources of ethical expertise can provide valuable insights and help leaders navigate challenging ethical decisions.

Regularly Evaluate and Review Ethical Practices:

Continuously assess and review the organization's ethical practices and policies to ensure that they remain aligned with the pursuit of the vision. Regularly evaluate the impact of decisions on ethics and make necessary adjustments to maintain ethical standards.

Lead by Example:

As a leader, it is crucial to lead by example and demonstrate ethical behavior in all actions and decisions. When leaders prioritize ethics and consistently act in an ethical manner, it sets the tone for the entire organization and encourages others to do the same.

Consider Long-Term Sustainability:

When pursuing a vision, consider the long-term sustainability of the organization and its impact on the environment, society, and future generations. Incorporate sustainability principles into the vision and strive to create a positive and lasting impact.

****

By actively balancing the pursuit of a vision with ethical considerations, leaders can ensure that their actions and decisions align with their values and contribute to the greater good. This balance not only strengthens the organization's reputation and stakeholder relationships but also creates a sustainable and responsible path toward achieving the vision.

Building trust and credibility through transparent and ethical practices is crucial for any individual or organization. Here are some strategies to achieve this:

Open and Honest Communication:

Foster a culture of open and honest communication by providing accurate and timely information to stakeholders. Be transparent about your intentions, actions, and decisions, and address any concerns or questions openly and honestly. This transparency builds trust and shows a commitment to ethical practices.

Consistency in Actions and Words:

Align your actions with your words to build credibility. Ensure that your behaviors and decisions reflect the values and principles you communicate. Consistency demonstrates integrity and reinforces trustworthiness.

Respect for Confidentiality and Privacy:

Respect for the confidentiality and privacy of individuals and organizations. Safeguard sensitive information and handle it responsibly. This demonstrates your commitment to ethical practices and builds trust with stakeholders.

Compliance with Laws and Regulations:

Adhere to all applicable laws, regulations, and industry standards. Ensure that your practices are in line with legal and ethical requirements. This demonstrates a commitment to ethical conduct and builds credibility with stakeholders.

Ethical Decision-Making:

Make ethical considerations a priority when making decisions. Consider the potential impact on stakeholders, society, and the environment. Seek diverse perspectives and opinions to make informed ethical decisions. This demonstrates a commitment to ethical practices and builds trust and credibility.

Accountability and Responsibility:

Take ownership of your actions and decisions. If mistakes are made, acknowledge them, take responsibility, and take appropriate steps to rectify the situation. Being accountable demonstrates integrity and builds trust and credibility.

Social and Environmental Responsibility:

Incorporate social and environmental responsibility into your practices. Consider the impact of your actions on society and the environment, take steps to minimize negative impacts, and contribute positively to the community. This demonstrates a commitment to ethical practices and builds trust and credibility.

Stakeholder Engagement:

Engage with stakeholders and involve them in decision-making processes. Seek their input, listen to their concerns, and address them transparently and ethically. This shows that you value their perspectives and builds trust and credibility.

Ethical Leadership:

Lead by example and demonstrate ethical behavior in all aspects of your work. Act with integrity, fairness, and respect for others. This sets the tone for the organization and encourages ethical practices among employees and stakeholders.

Continuous Improvement:

Regularly assess and evaluate your practices to identify areas for improvement. Seek feedback from stakeholders and make necessary adjustments to ensure ongoing transparency and ethical conduct. This demonstrates a commitment to continuous improvement and builds trust and credibility.

****

By incorporating these strategies into your practices, you can build trust and credibility by demonstrating transparency, integrity, and a commitment to ethical conduct. This, in turn, strengthens relationships with stakeholders and enhances your reputation as a trustworthy and ethical individual or organization.

8

Embracing Innovation and Embracing the Future

Embracing a mindset of continuous improvement and innovation is essential for personal and professional growth. Here are some ways to foster this mindset:

Embrace a Growth Mindset:

Adopt a mindset that believes in the potential for growth and improvement. See challenges and failures as opportunities to learn and develop. Embrace a positive attitude towards change and see it as a chance for innovation.

Seek Feedback:

Actively seek feedback from colleagues, mentors, and customers. Feedback provides valuable insights into areas where improvement and innovation are needed. Embrace constructive criticism and use it as a catalyst for growth.

Set Goals:

Set clear and achievable goals that push you outside of your comfort zone. Break down these goals into smaller milestones to track progress. Regularly evaluate and adjust your goals to ensure they align with your vision and aspirations.

Foster a Learning Culture:

Encourage a culture of continuous learning and development within your organization or team. Provide opportunities for training, workshops, and knowledge-sharing sessions. Encourage employees to pursue professional development and stay updated on industry trends.

Embrace Failure as a Learning Opportunity:

View failure as a stepping stone towards improvement and innovation. Analyze failures to identify areas for improvement and implement changes accordingly. Encourage experimentation and risk-taking, knowing that failures can provide valuable lessons.

Encourage Creativity and Collaboration:

Foster an environment that encourages creativity and collaboration. Create spaces for brainstorming, idea sharing, and cross-functional collaboration. Encourage diverse perspectives and foster an inclusive environment where everyone feels comfortable contributing their ideas.

Stay Informed:

Stay up to date with industry trends, technological advancements, and best practices. Regularly invest time in research and reading to broaden your knowledge and stay ahead of the curve. Attend conferences, webinars, and networking events to connect with industry experts.

Embrace Technology and Automation:

Explore how technology and automation can streamline processes, improve efficiency, and drive innovation. Stay open to adopting new tools and technologies that can enhance productivity and enable you to deliver better results.

Encourage Continuous Improvement Conversations:

Foster a culture where continuous improvement is a regular topic of conversation. Encourage team members to share ideas, suggestions, and innovative solutions. Create forums or platforms for open dialogue and collaboration.

Celebrate Successes:

Recognize and celebrate achievements and successes along the way. Acknowledge the efforts and contributions of individuals and teams who embrace a mindset of continuous improvement and innovation. This recognition encourages and motivates others to follow suit.

By embracing a mindset of continuous improvement and innovation, you create an environment that encourages growth, creativity, and progress. This mindset not only enhances personal and professional development but also drives positive change and success within your organization or team.

****

Nurturing a culture of experimentation and learning from failure is crucial for fostering innovation and continuous improvement within an organization or team.

Here are some ways to create such a culture:

Encourage Risk-Taking:

Create an environment where employees feel empowered to take risks and try new ideas without fear of failure. Encourage calculated risks and provide support and resources to mitigate potential negative outcomes.

Celebrate Learning, not just Success:

Shift the focus from solely celebrating success to also recognizing the value of learning and growth. Encourage individuals and teams to share what they have learned from failures and celebrate the lessons gained from those experiences.

Provide Psychological Safety:

Foster an environment where employees feel safe to share their ideas, take risks, and make mistakes. Encourage open communication, active listening, and non-judgmental feedback. Create an atmosphere where everyone's opinions are respected and valued.

Set Learning Goals:

Encourage individuals and teams to set learning goals alongside performance goals. This promotes a mindset of continuous improvement and encourages experimentation to achieve those goals.

Implement Post-Mortem Reviews:

After a project or initiative concludes, conduct post-mortem reviews to analyze what worked well and what didn't. Encourage open and honest discussions about failures and challenges faced. Use these reviews to identify areas for improvement and implement changes in future projects.

Provide Resources for Learning:

Offer learning opportunities such as workshops, training programs, and access to industry experts. Encourage employees to pursue continuous learning and provide resources to support their professional development.

Lead by Example:

Leaders should demonstrate their willingness to take risks and learn from failures. Share stories of personal failures and the lessons learned from them. This helps create a culture where failure is seen as a stepping stone towards success.

Encourage Experimentation:

Set aside time and resources for employees to experiment with new ideas and approaches. Create a process for testing and evaluating these experiments and encourage sharing the learnings with the broader team.

Foster Collaboration and Knowledge-Sharing:

Encourage cross-functional collaboration and create platforms for sharing knowledge and best practices. Encourage employees to learn from each other's failures and successes, fostering a culture of continuous learning.

Recognize and Reward Learning and Growth:

Recognize and reward individuals and teams who demonstrate a commitment to experimentation and learning. Celebrate both successful outcomes and the effort put into learning from failures.

By nurturing a culture of experimentation and learning from failure, you create an environment that encourages innovation, creativity, and continuous improvement. However, this culture enables individuals and teams to push boundaries, learn from their experiences, and ultimately drive positive change and growth within the organization.

****

Anticipating and adapting to future trends and disruptions is essential for organizations to stay competitive and relevant in a rapidly changing world.

Here are some strategies to help anticipate and adapt to future trends and disruptions:

Stay Informed:

Continuously monitor and analyze industry trends, technological advancements, and global developments that may impact your industry. Stay updated through industry reports, market research, news sources, and networking with industry experts.

Foster a Culture of Innovation:

Encourage a mindset of curiosity, creativity, and innovation within your organization. Create channels for employees to share ideas and insights and provide resources for experimentation and prototyping.

Conduct Scenario Planning:

Develop multiple scenarios of potential future outcomes based on different trends and disruptions. Consider both optimistic and pessimistic scenarios to understand the range of possibilities. This helps identify potential risks and opportunities.

Engage with Customers and Stakeholders:

Regularly engage with customers, partners, suppliers, and other stakeholders to understand their needs, expectations, and preferences. Use feedback and insights to inform your decision-making and adapt your strategies accordingly.

Embrace Technology and Digital Transformation:

Embrace emerging technologies and invest in digital transformation initiatives that can help your organization stay agile and adapt to future disruptions. Explore opportunities in areas such as artificial intelligence, automation, data analytics, and cloud computing.

Build a Diverse and Agile Workforce:

Foster a diverse and inclusive workforce that brings together different perspectives and expertise. Encourage continuous learning and upskilling to ensure your employees are equipped to adapt to changing trends and technologies.

Collaborate with External Partners:

Collaborate with external partners, such as startups, research institutions, and industry experts, to tap into their expertise and stay ahead of emerging trends. Partnering with innovative organizations can provide new insights and opportunities for collaboration.

Develop a Flexible and Adaptable Strategy:

Build flexibility into your strategic planning process to account for potential disruptions and changing market conditions. Regularly review and update your strategy based on new information and insights.

Invest in Research and Development:

Allocate resources for research and development activities to explore new technologies, business models, and market opportunities. This investment can help you stay at the forefront of innovation and adapt to future disruptions.

Monitor and Learn from Competitors:

Keep a close eye on your competitors and analyze their strategies, innovations, and responses to industry trends. Learn from their successes and failures to inform you of your own approach.

By actively anticipating and adapting to future trends and disruptions, organizations can position themselves to seize opportunities, mitigate risks, and maintain a competitive edge in an ever-changing business landscape. It requires a proactive approach, continuous learning, and a willingness to embrace change and innovation.

9

Sustaining Visionary Leadership

Sustaining the vision over the long term requires careful planning, strong leadership, and consistent execution.

Here are some strategies to help sustain the vision and ensure its longevity:

Clearly Communicate and Reinforce the Vision:

Ensure that the vision is clearly articulated and understood by everyone in the organization. Regularly communicate the vision and its importance to all stakeholders, including employees, customers, and partners. Reinforce the vision through consistent messaging and actions.

Align Goals and Actions with the Vision:

Ensure that the goals, strategies, and actions of the organization are aligned with the overall vision. Regularly review and evaluate progress towards the vision and adjust as needed. Keep the vision at the forefront of decision-making processes.

Develop a Strong Organizational Culture:

Foster a culture that supports and reinforces the vision. Encourage values and behaviors that are aligned with the vision, such as innovation, collaboration, and customer-centricity. Recognize and reward employees who demonstrate behaviors that contribute to the vision.

Empower and Engage Employees:

Empower employees to contribute to their vision by providing them with the necessary resources, autonomy, and support. Encourage employee involvement and participation in decision-making processes. Foster a sense of ownership and pride in the vision.

Continuously Adapt and Innovate:

Stay agile and adaptable in the face of changing market conditions, technological advancements, and customer needs. Encourage a culture of continuous learning and improvement. Foster innovation and experimentation to ensure the vision remains relevant and competitive.

Invest in Leadership Development:

Develop and nurture strong leaders who can champion the vision and inspire others. Provide leadership development programs and opportunities for growth. Ensure that leaders at all levels of the organization are aligned with the vision and equipped to drive its implementation.

Monitor and Measure Progress:

Establish key performance indicators (KPIs) and metrics to track progress towards the vision. Regularly monitor and review performance against these metrics. Use data and insights to identify areas for improvement and make informed decisions.

Foster Collaboration and Partnerships:

Collaborate with external stakeholders, such as customers, suppliers, industry associations, and community organizations, to advance the vision. Seek opportunities for partnerships and alliances that can help achieve the vision more effectively.

Anticipate and Manage Risks:

Identify potential risks and challenges that may hinder the realization of the vision. Develop risk mitigation strategies and contingency plans. Regularly assess and monitor risks to ensure proactive management.

Celebrate Milestones and Successes:

Recognize and celebrate milestones and successes along the journey towards the vision. This helps to maintain motivation, momentum, and engagement among employees and stakeholders.

By implementing these strategies, organizations can sustain their vision over the long term, ensuring that it remains relevant, inspiring, and achievable. However, it requires a commitment to ongoing communication, alignment, adaptation, and continuous improvement.

****

Developing successors and cultivating a pipeline of visionary leaders is essential for the long-term success of any organization. Here are some strategies to help in this process:

Identify and Nurture Potential Leaders:

Keep an eye out for employees who demonstrate potential leadership qualities, such as strong communication skills, problem-solving abilities, and a passion for the organization's vision. Provide them with opportunities for growth and development, such as mentoring, coaching, and training programs.

Create Leadership Development Programs:

Establish formal leadership development programs that provide aspiring leaders with the skills, knowledge, and experiences they need to succeed. These programs can include workshops, seminars, rotational assignments, and cross-functional projects. Tailor the programs to address specific leadership competencies and align them with the organization's vision and values.

Provide Mentoring and Coaching:

Pair aspiring leaders with experienced mentors who can provide guidance, support, and valuable insights. Mentors can help develop leadership capabilities, offer advice, and share their own experiences.

Additionally, consider providing coaching to help leaders identify and overcome development areas while building upon their strengths.

Encourage Continuous Learning and Growth:

Foster a culture of continuous learning and growth within the organization. Provide resources and opportunities for leaders to expand their knowledge and skills through workshops, conferences, online courses, and industry events. Encourage them to stay updated on the latest trends and best practices in their respective fields.

Offer Stretch Assignments and Opportunities:

Provide aspiring leaders with challenging assignments that push them out of their comfort zones and allow them to develop new skills and competencies. These stretch assignments can be cross-functional projects, leadership roles in task forces or committees, or special initiatives that align with the organization's strategic goals.

Promote a Culture of Innovation and Creativity:

Encourage leaders to think outside the box, take risks, and embrace innovation. Provide them with the freedom and resources to explore new ideas and solutions. Foster an environment where failure is seen as an opportunity for learning and growth.

Foster a Diverse and Inclusive Leadership Pipeline:

Ensure that the leadership pipeline reflects the diversity of the organization and its stakeholders. Create opportunities for individuals from underrepresented groups to develop their leadership skills and advance within the organization. Encourage diversity of thought and perspective in leadership positions.

Succession Planning and Talent Management:

Implement a robust succession planning process that identifies potential successors for key leadership roles. Continuously assess the readiness and potential of high-potential employees and provide them with the necessary development opportunities. Invest in talent management practices focus on attracting, retaining, and developing top talent.

Encourage Networking and Collaboration:

Facilitate opportunities for aspiring leaders to connect with their peers, both within and outside the organization. Encourage participation in industry associations, professional networks, and leadership forums. These connections can provide valuable insights, support, and learning opportunities.

Lead by Example:

Finally, leaders at all levels of the organization should embody the qualities and behaviors they expect from future leaders. Demonstrate a commitment to the organization's vision, values, and culture. Be accessible, approachable, and transparent in your leadership style.

By implementing these strategies, organizations can develop successors and cultivate a pipeline of visionary leaders who can drive the organization forward and sustain its vision over the long term. It requires a proactive approach to leadership development, a commitment to continuous learning, and a culture that values and nurtures future leaders.

****

The legacy of a visionary leader refers to the lasting impact they leave behind through their actions, decisions, and influence. A visionary leader's legacy is often characterized by their ability to inspire and motivate others, their innovative ideas and approaches, and their long-term contributions to the organization or community they serve.

Here are some aspects that contribute to the legacy of a visionary leader:

Transformational Change:

Visionary leaders have a unique ability to envision a future that is different from the status quo. They inspire and rally others around a shared vision, driving transformative change within their organization or community. Their ability to articulate a compelling vision and create a sense of purpose leads to meaningful and sustainable change.

Innovation and Creativity:

Visionary leaders are often known for their innovative thinking and willingness to challenge conventional wisdom. They encourage a culture of creativity and experimentation, fostering an environment where new ideas can thrive. Their ability to identify emerging trends and capitalize on new opportunities drives innovation within their organization or industry.

Empowering Others:

Visionary leaders understand the importance of empowering others and building strong teams. They delegate authority and provide individuals with the autonomy and resources needed to succeed. By fostering a culture of trust and collaboration, they inspire their team members to reach their full potential and contribute to the overall success of the organization.

Long-Term Vision:

A visionary leader's impact extends beyond their immediate tenure. They have a long-term perspective and make decisions that prioritize the organization's future sustainability and growth. Their strategic thinking and ability to anticipate and navigate challenges ensure the organization's continued success even after they have moved on.

Legacy of Values:

Visionary leaders often leave behind a legacy of values that shape the organization's culture and guide decision-making. They set high ethical standards and lead by example, instilling a sense of integrity, accountability, and transparency. These values become embedded in the organization's DNA and continue to influence its actions long after the leader has departed.

Mentorship and Development:

Visionary leaders invest in the development of others. They recognize the importance of mentorship and actively support the growth and advancement of their team members. By nurturing and developing future leaders, they leave a lasting impact on the organization's leadership pipeline, ensuring its continued success in the future.

Social Impact:

Visionary leaders often extend their influence beyond their organization and make a positive impact on society. They champion social causes, promote diversity and inclusion, and contribute to the well-being of their community. Their actions inspire others to follow in their footsteps, creating a ripple effect of positive change.

Overall, the legacy of a visionary leader is characterized by their ability to inspire, drive transformative changes, and leave a lasting impact on their organization, industry, and community. Their visionary thinking, innovative approaches, and commitment to empowering others create a legacy that extends far beyond their time in leadership.

10

The Power of Being a Visionary Leader

Numerous visionary leaders throughout history have made transformative impacts in various fields.

Here are a few success stories that highlight the visionary leadership and their lasting impact:

Steve Jobs (Apple Inc.):

Steve Jobs co-founded Apple Inc. and played a pivotal role in revolutionizing the technology industry. His visionary leadership led to the creation of game-changing products like the iPhone, iPad, and Macintosh computers. Jobs' relentless pursuit of innovation and emphasis on design aesthetics transformed Apple into one of the most valuable and influential companies in the world, setting new standards for the consumer electronics industry.

Nelson Mandela (South Africa):

Nelson Mandela was a visionary leader who played a key role in ending apartheid in South Africa. His unwavering commitment to justice, equality, and reconciliation helped dismantle the oppressive system of racial segregation and laid the foundation for a democratic and inclusive South Africa. Mandela's leadership and moral courage continue to inspire people around the world in the fight against injustice and oppression.

Elon Musk (Tesla, SpaceX):

Elon Musk is a visionary entrepreneur known for his transformative impact in the fields of electric vehicles and space exploration. Through his companies, Tesla and SpaceX, Musk has been instrumental in driving the adoption of sustainable transportation and advancing the possibilities of space travel. His vision for a sustainable future and his relentless pursuit of technological breakthroughs have revolutionized industries and inspired a new generation of innovators.

Malala Yousafzai (Education Activist):

Malala Yousafzai is a Pakistani education activist who became a global symbol of the fight for girls' education. Despite facing threats from the Taliban, she continued to advocate for the right to education for all children, especially girls. Her courage and determination led to international recognition, and she became the youngest Nobel Prize laureate. Malala's advocacy has sparked conversations and initiatives worldwide, highlighting the importance of education in empowering individuals and promoting social change.

Mahatma Gandhi (Indian Independence Movement):

Mahatma Gandhi was a visionary leader who played a pivotal role in India's struggle for independence from British rule. Through his philosophy of nonviolent resistance, Gandhi inspired millions of people to peacefully resist oppression and fight for their rights. His leadership and principles continue to motivate movements for social justice, civil rights, and peace across the globe.

****

Embracing one's own visionary leadership potential can be a transformative journey that not only creates personal growth but also inspires others.

Here are some ways to encourage individuals to embrace their visionary leadership potential:

Self-reflection and Discovery:

Encourage individuals to engage in self-reflection to understand their passions, values, and unique strengths. By exploring their own interests and aspirations, they can gain clarity on what they truly care about and envision for themselves and the world.

Setting Audacious Goals:

Encourage individuals to set audacious goals that challenge the status quo and push the boundaries of what is possible. By encouraging them to think big and aim high, they can tap into their visionary thinking and unleash their full potential.

Cultivating an Innovative Mindset:

Inspire individuals to embrace an innovative mindset that encourages them to think outside the box, question conventional wisdom, and seek creative solutions to problems. Encourage them to embrace failure as a learning opportunity and adopt a growth mindset that fosters continuous learning and improvement.

Building a Supportive Network:

Surrounding oneself with like-minded and supportive individuals can provide encouragement, inspiration, and valuable feedback. Encourage individuals to seek mentors, join communities of like-minded individuals, and collaborate with others who share their vision.

Taking Calculated Risks:

Encourage individuals to step outside their comfort zones and take calculated risks. Embracing uncertainty and overcoming fear can lead to new opportunities and innovative breakthroughs. Encourage them to learn from failures and setbacks and to persevere in the face of challenges.

Fostering Empathy and Inclusivity:

Remind individuals of the importance of empathy and inclusiveness in visionary leadership. Encourage them to consider the needs and perspectives of others and to strive for social impact that benefits a diverse range of individuals and communities.

Leading by Example:

Inspire individuals to lead by example and demonstrate their own visionary leadership potential in their actions and decisions. Encourage them to be authentic, transparent, and ethical in their leadership approach, inspiring others to follow suit.

By encouraging individuals to tap into their own visionary leadership potential, we can create a ripple effect of positive change and inspire others to embrace their own unique visions and make a difference in the world.

These success stories demonstrate how visionary leaders can envision a better future, inspire others, and drive transformative changes in their respective fields. Their lasting impact continues to shape the world we live in today and serves as a testament to the power of visionary leadership.

****

The collective power of visionary leaders is instrumental in creating a better future for society. When visionary leaders come together and unite their efforts, they can drive significant positive change and shape a brighter future.

Here are some key aspects of the collective power of visionary leaders:

Shared Vision:

Visionary leaders share a common vision of a better future. They have a clear understanding of the challenges and opportunities that lie ahead and are committed to creating positive change. By aligning their visions, they can create a unified force that amplifies their impact.

Collaboration and Cooperation:

Visionary leaders recognize the value of collaboration and cooperation. They understand that by working together, they can leverage their collective strengths, resources, and expertise to address complex problems more effectively. Collaboration allows for the sharing of ideas, the pooling of resources, and the ability to tackle larger-scale initiatives.

Synergy of Ideas:

When visionary leaders come together, they bring diverse perspectives, experiences, and ideas to the table. This diversity of thought fosters innovation and creativity, leading to the development of more robust and comprehensive solutions. The synergy of ideas generated through collaboration can lead to breakthrough innovations and transformative changes.

Influence and Inspiration:

Visionary leaders can inspire and influence others. By working collectively, they can inspire a broader audience, including other leaders, organizations, and communities, to embrace their own visionary potential and contribute to creating a better future. Their influence can extend beyond their immediate sphere of influence, creating a ripple effect of positive change.

Amplified Impact:

The collective power of visionary leaders amplifies their impact. Through collaboration, they can tackle larger-scale initiatives, address systemic issues, and effect widespread change. Their combined efforts can lead to the implementation of policies, programs, and initiatives that create a ripple effect, benefiting society.

Long-Term Sustainability:

Visionary leaders understand the importance of long-term sustainability. They prioritize strategies and initiatives that not only address immediate challenges but also lay the foundation for a sustainable future. By working collectively, they can develop and implement sustainable solutions that ensure the longevity of positive change.

Empowering Future Leaders:

Visionary leaders have a responsibility to empower and nurture the next generation of leaders. By working collectively, they can provide mentorship, guidance, and opportunities for emerging leaders to develop their own visionary leadership potential. This ensures the continuity of efforts to create a better future.

****

In conclusion, the collective power of visionary leaders is a driving force in creating a better future. By leveraging their shared vision, collaborating, and inspiring others, they can amplify their impact, foster innovation, and drive transformative changes that benefit families, communities, businesses, and society.

Isaiah Ike Johnson's U.S. Marine Military Service

Ranks:

- Private (E-1)
- Private First Class (E-2)
- Lance Corporal (E-3)
- Corporal (E-4) Sergeant (E-5)
- Staff Sergeant (E-6)
- Gunnery Sergeant (E-7)
- Warrant Officer (W-1) and (W-2)
- First Lieutenant (0-2)
- Captain (O-3)
- Major (O-4)

Jobs:

- Military Occupational Specialty
- Infantry Machine Gunner
- Infantry Training Instructor
- Drill Instructor
- College Naval Reserve Officer Training Corps Instructor
- Military Policeman
- Bulk Fuel Officer

- Engineer Maintenance Officer
- Food Service Officer

Assignments:

- Parris Island SC - Squad Leader in boot Camp and Infantry Training School
- Camp Pendleton CA - Infantry Training Center
- Okinawa Japan - Infantry Squad Leader, 3rd Battalion 4th Marines
- Camp Lejeune, NC - 2nd Battalion 8th Marines, Instructor Infantry Training Center
- Camp Giger, NC - Infantry Training School
- Parris Island, SC - Drill Instructor, 3rd Recruit Battalion, Marine Corps Recruit Depot
- Quantico, VA - Military Drill Instructor, Officer Candidate School
- Columbia, MO - Assistant Military Officer Instructor, University of Missouri
- Camp Lejeune, NC - Military Police Platoon Sergeant, and Director of Support Services Division, Provost Marshall Officer
- Iwakuni Japan - Special Services Chief, Marine Corps, Air Station
- Quantico, VA - Warrant Officer Bulk Fuel Student at the Marine Corps Officer's Basic School
- Fort Lee, VA - Bulk Fuel Quartermaster School Student
- Camp Lejeune, NC - Operation Officer, Bulk Fuel, Company, Adjutant, Eighth Engineer Support Battalion, Student Engineer School, Court House Bay
- Camp Lejeune, NC - Maintenance Management Officer, Support Company; Executive Officer, 8th Engineer Support Battalion

- Fort Lee, VA - Food Service and Commissary Course, Quartermaster School
- Camp Johnson, NC - Senior Course, Food Service School
- Camp Pendleton CA - Food Service Officer 1st Marine Division
- Desert Shield and Desert Storm - Food Service Officer; 1st Marine Division
- Parris Island, SC - Food Service Officer, Marine Corps Recruit Depot
- Quantico, VA - Food Service Officer, Marine Corps Base
- Fort Lee, VA - Commanding Officer of Marine Corps, Food Service School, Quartermaster School

Education:

- Bachelor of Arts Degree, psychology, Columbia College, Columbia, Missouri
- Bachelor of Arts Degree, 1982, Criminal Justice, Columbia College, Columbia, Missouri
- Master of Science Degree, Human Resources Management, Golden Gate University, San Francisco, CA

Personal Military Awards:

- Bronze Star
- Meritorious Service Medal w/gold star
- Navy Achievement Medal
- Johnson, Isaiah. From Average to Excellent: How I Transformed My Dreams into Goals, Goals Into Plans, and Plans Into Success (p. 143). Kindle Edition.

Made in the USA
Columbia, SC
09 January 2025

9e6b7f68-e0a6-43c1-b475-0d8ad8f80502R01